LAMENTATIONS: HOW CHRIST LIFTS THE BURDEN OF SIN AND SORROW

Jonathan Gibson

STUDY GUIDE WITH LEADER'S NOTES

New Growth Press
newgrowthpress.com

In memoriam

Frances Maud Roberts
(1907–1997)
My grandmother—sufferer and saint

****

New Growth Press, Greensboro, NC 27401
newgrowthpress.com

Cover Design: Faceout Studio, faceoutstudio.com
Interior Typesetting and Ebook: Lisa Parnell, lparnellbookservices.com
Exercises and Application Questions: Kristen J. Hsu

ISBN: 978-1-64507-515-8 (print)
ISBN: 978-1-64507-516-5 (ebook)

Printed in the United States of America

29 28 27 26 25 1 2 3 4 5

CONTENTS

THE WORLD OF LAMENTATIONS 1

INTRODUCTION 3

Lesson 1 - **Why Lamentations?** 6
Text: *2 Kings 25:1–21 and Deuteronomy 28:1–2 and 15–19*
Article: *Learning from Lament to Lament*
Exercise: *Journeying with Jesus into the Valley of Lament*

Lesson 2 - **Who Will Save Us from Judgment?** 18
Text: *Lamentations 1*
Article: *Where Do You Go in Your Sin and Misery?*
Exercise: *Learning to Lament, Turning to Jesus*

Lesson 3 - **Standing Where the Fire Has Already Been** 30
Text: *Lamentations 2*
Article: *Living in Between God's Past and Future Days of Judgment*
Exercise: *Pour Out Your Heart*

Lesson 4 - **A Journey Toward Hope** 39
Text: *Lamentations 3*
Article: *Great Is Thy Faithfulness*
Exercise: *Naming God in the Darkness*

Lesson 5 - **The Cup Shall Pass** 49
Text: *Lamentations 4*
Article: *The Devastating Effects of God's Judgment*
Exercise: *How the Cup of Salvation Changes Our Lives*

Lesson 6 - **Comfort in Suffering** 58
Text: *Lamentations 5*
Article: *Living in Limbo*
Exercise: *Looking to Jesus in Our Time of Suffering*

LEADER'S NOTES 69

THE WORLD OF LAMENTATIONS

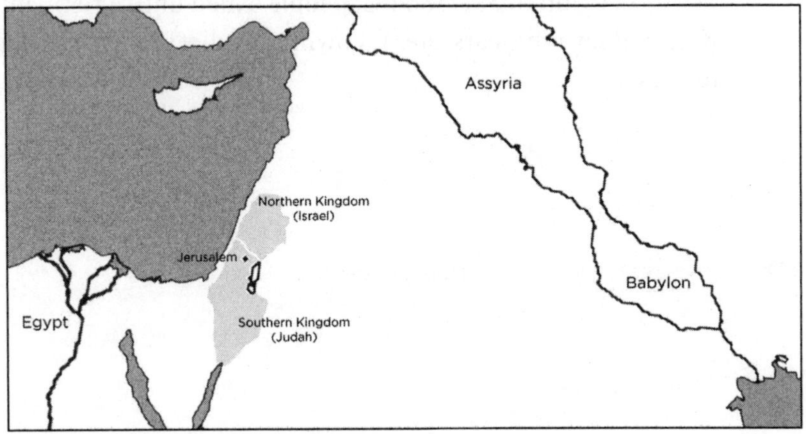

THE NORTHERN KINGDOM

- Called Israel, or sometimes Ephraim after its most notable tribe
- Steeped in idol worship since separating from the Southern Kingdom two centuries before
- Fell to Assyria in 722 BC as judgment for its unfaithfulness; people deported or otherwise assimilated into surrounding cultures

THE SOUTHERN KINGDOM

- Called Judah after its most notable tribe, or sometimes Jerusalem after its capital city; in the book of Lamentations, Jerusalem (as the capital) stands for Judah (the nation)
- Original and primary audience of Isaiah's message

- More faithful to God than the Northern Kingdom, but had periods of unchecked sin and idolatry deserving judgment
- Invaded by Assyria in 701 BC, but temporarily spared by God's intervention under the reign of the godly King Hezekiah
- Fell to Babylon in 587/586 BC; people exiled until a remnant returned seventy years later following an edict by Cyrus, King of Persia

INTRODUCTION

To many modern Western Christians, the idea of lament is unfamiliar. The practice of lament is not really something we do. And so it's easy to pass over a somber book like Lamentations for something more familiar, and frankly more cheerful. Why study Lamentations?

The preacher of Ecclesiastes said,

> It is better to go to the house of mourning
>   than to go to the house of feasting,
> for this is the end of all mankind,
>   and the living will lay it to heart. (7:2)

What a strange idea: It is *better* to go to the house of mourning than to the house of feasting? That's like saying it's better to attend a funeral than a birthday party. Or that it's better to go to the mortuary than to a Thanksgiving dinner. Why? Because

> The heart of the wise is in the house of mourning,
>   but the heart of fools is in the house of mirth. (7:4)

The book of Lamentations invites us into the house of mourning to gain a heart of wisdom. God, in his wisdom and love for us, has placed a book in the Bible that teaches us about lament so that we might lament, so that we might gain a heart of wisdom.

If you live long enough in this world, you will experience hard times, sad times, tragic times, confusing times. A book like Lamentations gives us language that we can use to express our feelings and sorrows to God in those times.

Throughout Lamentations, as with the other studies in this series, you will be encouraged to look to Jesus and trust in him. As you participate in this study together as a group, you will not only encounter the suffering of Jerusalem when the city was destroyed, but you'll also see the suffering of Jesus at the cross. You'll listen in as a community brings their suffering to the Lord, and you'll be invited to voice your own suffering to our Savior. Through this study of Lamentations, you'll see more of the story of how Christ lifts the burden of sin and sorrow on the cross, and how he continues to lift our burden as we draw near to him.

HOW TO USE THIS STUDY

This study guide is designed to help you learn from Lamentations within a small group. As your group engages in the topic of lament, you will likely find that some are seasoned sufferers, some are in the midst of suffering, and some are "gaining a heart of wisdom" to prepare for suffering that may come in the future. Pray for the Holy Spirit to work in your group. Make it a place where you are patient with those who need more time to process and sympathize with those who, like you, still struggle with suffering and sin. Such an approach reflects the burden-lifting Savior you'll encounter in your study.

Each participant should have one of these study guides to join in reading and be able to work through the exercises during that part of the study. The study leader should read through both the lesson and the leader's notes in the back of this book before each lesson begins. No other preparation or homework is required.

There are six lessons in this study guide. Each lesson will take about an hour to complete, perhaps a bit more if your group is large, and will include these elements:

BIG IDEA. This is a summary of the main point of the lesson.

BIBLE CONVERSATION. You will typically read a passage from Lamentations and discuss it. (In Lesson 1 you'll read other passages for background context.) As the heading suggests, the Bible conversation questions are intended to spark a conversation rather than generate correct answers. The leader's notes at the back of this book provide some insights, but don't just turn there for the "right answer." At times you may want to see what the notes say, but always try to answer for yourself first by thinking about the Bible passage.

ARTICLE. This is the main teaching section of the lesson.

DISCUSSION. The discussion questions following the article will help you apply the teaching to your life.

EXERCISE. The exercise is a section you will complete on your own during group time. You can write in the book if that helps you. You will then share some of what you learned with the group. If the group is large, it may help to split up to share the results of the exercise and to pray, so that everyone has a better opportunity to participate.

WRAP-UP AND PRAYER. Prayer is a critical part of the lesson because your spiritual growth will happen through God's work in you, not by your self-effort. As you study Lamentations, you are invited to "Pour out your heart like water before the presence of the Lord" (Lamentations 2:19). Make this time of prayer an important part of your group dialogue—it is where the truth that Christ lifts the burden of sin and sorrow can become real in your life!

God's Word is like a "deep mine," with "jewels rich and rare hidden in its mighty depths."[1] As you search and study Lamentations, you will find God's steadfast love, unending mercies, and great faithfulness. And you will see how Christ lifts the burden of sin and sorrow. Keep your eyes open for these jewels!

---

1. From the hymn "Thy Word Is like a Garden, Lord," by Edwin Hodder (1863).

Lesson

1

WHY LAMENTATIONS?

BIG IDEA

Jesus walks with us as we journey into suffering and lament—even when our suffering, like Jerusalem's, comes as a result of our sin.

BIBLE CONVERSATION *20 MINUTES*

This is an introductory lesson in which we'll do an overview of Lamentations (in the Article) and look at the historical and theological context for the book (in the Bible Conversation).

It's helpful to understand the historical context for the book of Lamentations. The people of Judah experienced three waves of exilic removal to Babylon between 606–587 BC. The final wave resulted in the climactic and cataclysmic destruction of Jerusalem/Zion and, most significantly, the temple.[1]

Have someone read **2 Kings 25:1–21** aloud, or have a few readers take turns. Then discuss the questions below:

This historical text reads like a news report—it tells us what has happened. Lamentations is an emotional and Godward response to this event. How would you describe your own response to reading or

1. 2 Kings 25:1–21

watching the news? When do you have an emotional or prayerful response to current events? How would you describe that? How would you like to grow or change throughout this study?

It's important to see the theological context of the book if we are going to understand it properly. The devastating judgment that Jerusalem experienced had come to them not accidentally by blind fate, but by divine fiat. Judah and its city and temple were in the state they were in because of their own sin. This was a reality they had to face up to, but when they did—as hard as that reality was—there was hope for them.[2] Judah had to realize that just as God had the power to punish them for their sin, so he had the power to restore them after they had sinned.

Deuteronomy 28 provides us with the theological context; in particular, it gives us the long list of curses (vv. 15–68) that are the backdrop to many of the curses experienced by the people of Judah in Lamentations.

Now have someone read **Deuteronomy 28:1–2 and 15–19** (notice that the curses continue through verse 68). Then discuss the question below:

Summarize, in your own words, the terms of the covenant: What do the people need to do, and what does God promise in response?

2. Lamentations 3:22–24

****

Next, take turns reading the article aloud, switching readers with each paragraph. Then discuss the questions that follow.

Lesson 1

ARTICLE

LEARNING FROM LAMENT TO LAMENT[3]

5 MINUTES

I don't think it would be an exaggeration to say that as a church living in the modern world, we don't really know what to do with a book like Lamentations. Traditionally, the book has been read in the Christian church during Holy Week. But unless you keep the church calendar, I doubt you have read the book of Lamentations on an annual basis every Easter season. If you read through the Bible each year, then you will have read it at some point in the year, but I wonder if you've known how to read it properly, how to understand it, how to set it within the Bible's grand storyline, and even what to do in response to reading it.

Perhaps we don't know what to do with it because our surrounding culture is a culture addicted to hedonism, to pleasure seeking. Technology and social media also mean we don't meditate on anything for more than a few seconds, never mind the topic of lament. We've all seen images of bloodshed and war on the news, but have they caused us to stop and offer up a prayer of lament? A technological

3. Mark Vroegop, *Dark Clouds, Deep Mercy: Discovering the Grace of Lament* (Crossway, 2019), 89. I am indebted to Vroegop for this concept.

age addicted to clicking, swiping, and scrolling doesn't lend itself to lamenting. Our culture is averse to any serious engagement with sin and death, with suffering and sorrow, and I think this has affected Christians more than we might like to think. We don't really know what to do with a book like Lamentations, which is full of relentless lament. If we're honest, lament is a lost discipline in the church at large.[4]

And yet **God wants his people to lament.** It's why he has dedicated a whole book in the Christian Scripture to this one subject—Lamentations—a book of laments. As such, it is a place to begin to learn how to lament.

The early church father Athanasius said, "The Scriptures speaks *to* us; but the Psalms speak *for* us."[5] I think that Lamentations does both—it speaks *to* us about lament, but it also speaks *for* us when we experience something terrible that causes us to lament.

As we begin this study on the book of Lamentations, let me invite you to learn from this book of laments so that you might know *how* to lament for the times when you will *need* to lament.

Let's consider a couple of things as we begin:

PATHOS (THE FEEL OF LAMENTATIONS)

Lamentations is full of pathos—it's full of emotion. One of the most moving books in the Bible, it serves as a fitting complement to Job or some of the psalms of lament.

Hear the depressing note expressed for a beloved city in its opening verse: "How lonely sits the city that was full of people!" (1:1). Or the pitiful cry of the lonely figure of chapter 3: "Remember my affliction

4. Mark Vroegop's book *Dark Clouds, Deep Mercy* is a helpful corrective.

5. Athanasius, *Letter to Marcellinus*, paraphrased in John Goldingay, *Psalms*, vol. 1, *Psalms 1–41* (Baker Academic, 2006), 23 (emphasis added).

and my wanderings, the wormwood and the gall!" (3:19). Or the impassioned plea of the exiled community in chapter 5: "Remember, O Lord, what has befallen us; look, and see our disgrace!" (v. 1). The words of this ancient book draw us in and stir our emotions and affections.

But its purpose was not simply to stir our emotions and affections—the purpose of the book is *to call God's exiled people to repentance for their sin and to hope in God's steadfast love for their forgiveness and restoration.*

The author of Lamentations seeks to express in words what that final destruction of city and temple meant for the people of God. Judah and its city and temple were in the state they were in because of their own sin. This was a reality they had to face up to, but when they did—as hard as that reality was—there was hope for them.[6]

Judah had to realize that just as God had the power to punish them for their sin, so he had the power to restore them after they had sinned. This is why the book ends:

> Restore us to yourself, O Lord, that we may be restored!
> Renew our days as of old—
> even though you have utterly rejected us,
> and remain exceedingly angry with us.
> (5:21–22, author's translation)

So that is the purpose of the book: to call God's exiled people to repentance for their sin and to hope in God's steadfast love for their forgiveness and restoration.

The suffering that Jerusalem-Judah experiences at the hand of the Lord is a result of their covenant unfaithfulness.[7] In this sense, there

---

6. Lamentations 3:22–24
7. See, for example, 1:5b, 14a, 18a.

is no real mystery to the suffering of Jerusalem-Judah compared to the book of Job. In the book of Job, Job is presented as an "innocent" sufferer; in Lamentations, Jerusalem-Judah is presented as a "guilty" sufferer. The suffering makes sense because it is a result of their sin.

And yet, the punishment from God still comes as something of a surprise, given what Jerusalem and her people meant to God.[8] In the Old Testament, especially in psalms like the Songs of Zion,[9] Zion is described as impenetrable and inviolable precisely because God was in her midst. This is what was so shocking to Jerusalem-Judah—the God who promised to be in the midst of her, like a shield protecting her from her enemies, became in her midst a fire destroying her.

How could this be? It was because of the covenant arrangement between God and Israel. We need to read Lamentations against the backdrop of Deuteronomy 28, where God had warned and threatened disaster on his people if they disobeyed him. Lamentations records just such a disaster because of their covenant unfaithfulness. What we see in Lamentations is the misery that Jerusalem-Judah experiences as a result of their sin.

CHRIST IN LAMENTATIONS

Lamentations presents us with the bad news of sin and judgment but also the good news of hope and deliverance according to God's steadfast love. However, connecting the book to Christ can be difficult. There are no predictive prophecies in the book, nothing that explains what the future Messiah will do. To find Christ in Lamentations, you have to look at people, things, and events (what biblical scholars call "types") that show us what the Messiah will be *like*—types such as the ruined temple,[10] or the prophet who weeps over the city that has

8. Lamentations 2:15; 4:20; 5:17–18
9. Psalms 46; 48; 76
10. John 2:19

rejected God,[11] or the city that is suffering, or the exile itself. Seeing these connections will enrich our understanding of the beauty and glory of Jesus as the great Man of Sorrows, who as the leader of God's people underwent great suffering for his people's sins. As we will see, Jesus is the ultimate prophet, priest, and king who suffers; the ultimate temple that is destroyed; the ultimate city that experiences God's wrath.

DISCUSSION *10 MINUTES*

What helpful models or experiences with lament have you seen or lived through? If the idea of lament is new to you, what is attractive about it?

If you or someone you know is in the midst of lament, how is it comforting to know that you are not alone—that Jesus experienced so much grief that he was known as the "Man of Sorrows"?

11. Matthew 23:37–38

Lesson 1

EXERCISE

JOURNEYING WITH JESUS INTO THE VALLEY OF LAMENT

20 MINUTES

The beginning of this study of Lamentations is like the start of a journey. We stand at the vista, looking down at the valley below. Jesus is our companion, inviting us, leading us, sojourning with us as we set out to travel together into the valley of lament.

In this exercise, you will consider what you bring with you as you start this journey—what is in your heart. You'll read four different "postures toward suffering" and circle the one that best describes your own heart's posture. Then you'll read a passage that reflects that posture and write out a prayer asking the Lord to meet you where you are and work in your heart.

You'll work through the exercise individually, and then you'll regather with your group to talk about how what you bring and what you hope for in this journey through Lamentations.

Ask the Spirit to search your heart as you embark on this journey in the land of lament. Pray Psalm 139:23–24:

Search me, O God, and know my heart!
  Try me and know my thoughts!
And see if there be any grievous way in me,
  and lead me in the way everlasting!

Ask the Spirit to reveal your heart's posture toward suffering and lament.

- Perhaps there are ways you are aloof and indifferent to the suffering of others—like reading devastating news and *not* bringing it to the Lord, or like the rich man with Lazarus (you may read Luke 16:19–20, and on to verse 31 if this posture resonates with you).
- Perhaps there are ways you are judgmental toward others in their suffering. Like the disciples who encountered the man born blind—quick to cast blame, slow to consider how the glory of God might be displayed (you may read John 9:1–3 and the entire chapter if this posture resonates with you).
- Perhaps you are just curious—eager to learn and to grow in dependence on Jesus in all circumstances. Bring your earnest desire to the Lord and ask him to be a leader and guide to you on this journey into Lamentations. (You may read Psalm 23:4 and ask the Lord—your shepherd who is with you in the valley—to help you know him, his presence, and his comfort better in your life and in suffering.)
- One more possibility: Perhaps, like Jerusalem, you share a sense of guilt for your own suffering.
    - Although it is certainly not the case that all suffering falls on someone who "got what they deserved," here in the book of Lamentations, Jerusalem was a "guilty" sufferer. The misery that Jerusalem laments is merited—the nation had broken covenant with God.

- Some of our deepest suffering is so painful not only because of the great loss, but also because we find fault in ourselves. There was some failure where we didn't do what we should have done. Something we might not have known at the time, but looking back with 20/20 hindsight, we see how we could have done something differently. Our own failure, mistake, or lack is woven into our lament.
- As you consider your own suffering, come to Jesus with your sin, with the ways you contributed to your suffering. His love for you also covers that. If this is you, stop here. Ask the Spirit to search you. Name the unnameable. Ask God to show you both the depths of your heart (or fault, sorrow, lack, regret, sin), but even more the depths of his love. You may read Romans 8:33–39.
- Rewrite verse 35, naming the ways you may have contributed to your suffering. Can those things separate you from the love of God?
- Look again to verse 37 for the resounding NO, and to verses 38–39 for the assurance that nothing you have done or failed to do, not even the deserved suffering you have brought on yourself, can separate you from the love of God in Christ.

Space to write out your prayer:

When the group is ready, share some of your responses. What posture toward suffering do you start with? In what ways do you hope to experience God's work in your heart through this study?

WRAP-UP AND PRAYER *10 MINUTES*

You are setting off on a countercultural journey into the house of mourning to gain a heart of wisdom. Each person in your group brings their own experiences and their own posture toward suffering. Pray together, asking for the Lord to lead your group—that you would learn *from* lament *to* lament. Ask the Spirit to open your eyes to see more of Christ, not only in the Scriptures, but also in your very lives.

Lesson

2

WHO WILL SAVE US FROM JUDGMENT?

BIG IDEA

Lament is the prayer we pray to Jesus "while living under the curse of sin."[1]

BIBLE CONVERSATION *20 MINUTES*

The author of Lamentations seeks to express in words what the exile to Babylon and destruction of the city and temple meant for the people of God. In doing so, his purpose is to call God's exiled people to repentance for their sin and to hope in God's steadfast love for their forgiveness and restoration.

Lamentations opens with the city, personified as Woman Jerusalem or Lady Zion, recounting her grief and with no one to comfort her. Jerusalem here represents the whole nation of Israel—her sorrow is the nation's sorrow. The terms *Jerusalem*, *Zion*, *Judah*, *Israel*, and *Jacob* are used interchangeably.

---

1. "Lament is the song we sing while living under the curse of sin," Vroegop, *Deep Clouds, Deep Mercy* (99).

The Old Testament image of God's relationship with Israel as that of husband and wife sets the backdrop for Lamentations 1. The city is personified as a lonely, bereaved, enslaved woman who has prostituted herself with other lovers. It is not that God her husband has died, but rather that he has forsaken her. She has become estranged from him because of her unfaithful ways with the gods of other nations.

Lamentations 1 can be broken into two parts:

- The first half (vv. 1–11) is a lament for Jerusalem. This is written from the voice of the prophet, who is part of the community experiencing affliction from God.
- The second half (beginning with v. 12) is a lament to the Lord. The speaker here is the voice of Lady Jerusalem.

Have someone read **Lamentations 1:1–22** aloud, or have a few readers take turns. Then discuss the questions below:

The laments of Lamentations arise because of two realities that Jerusalem has experienced, both of which are common to us all: sin and its miserable consequences. Which examples of sin or the misery it creates stand out to you as particularly grievous or devastating?

Notice the repeated refrain, "There was no one to comfort her." How does having no one to comfort you make suffering worse?

How do you respond emotionally to this chapter, or what hard questions do you want answered going forward?

****

Now take turns reading the article aloud, switching readers with each paragraph. Then discuss the questions that follow.

Lesson

WHERE DO YOU GO IN YOUR SIN AND MISERY?

5 MINUTES

In this opening chapter of Lamentations, Jerusalem has sinned against God. With that sin comes God's curse and punishment. Where there is sin, there is suffering. Where there is sin, there is misery.

Of course, some care is needed here because, while we may experience suffering as a result of our own sins, not all suffering is directly related to our own sins. Jesus made that clear with the man born blind.[2] Here in Lamentations, the children who were led into captivity (v. 5) were not guilty of covenant unfaithfulness themselves, and yet they suffered for the sins of their parents.

This principle can ultimately be traced all the way back to the sin of our first father, Adam. Because of his rebellion against God, we all now live with the consequences of sin. In this respect, sin affects everything. So whatever suffering we experience in this life is related to sin in some way, either to our own sin or someone else's sin, but ultimately, to Adam's sin and the misery it brings.

2. John 9

What we will ultimately come to find is that just as sin and misery entered the world through one man, Adam, so also the cure for our sin and the comfort for our misery comes through one man, Jesus Christ.[3]

Notice the parallels between what Jerusalem experienced in her fall and what Jesus experienced on the cross. Like the weeping Lady Zion, Jesus wept over Jerusalem and over the death of Lazarus. He experienced betrayal from his friend Judas, who handed him over to his enemies.

On the cross, Jesus went into exile. He found no rest for his soul. While he hung there with his nakedness exposed to all, his enemies mocked him, gloating over his demise. He experienced desertion from his family and friends. He was distressed in his spirit.

Truly Jesus could say, "O Lord, behold my affliction, for the enemy has triumphed!" and, "Look, O Lord, and see, for I am despised" (vv. 9, 11). In the end, when Jesus cried the cry of dereliction, "My God, my God, why have you forsaken me?" (Mark 15:34), there was no one to comfort him. Even God was silent.

Jesus's sorrow was incomparable to all other sorrow as he received the wrath of God in those three hours of darkness on the cross. It was compounded by the thundering silence of heaven in response to his cry of dereliction: Is there any sorrow like my sorrow? Though innocent himself, on the cross he bore the yoke of transgressions for his people. The Lord provided no deliverer for him. With arms hung wide on the cross, no comforter came to revive his spirit.

In the bloody and beaten and abandoned Jerusalem, we see the bloody and beaten and abandoned Jesus. Jerusalem symbolized Judah; the princes and people of Judah typified Jesus. Jerusalem's destruction and exile is a window to Jesus's Golgotha; Judah's captivity, to Jesus's Calvary.

3. Romans 5:12–21

Yet, while Jerusalem's sufferings foreshadowed the sufferings of her King, there is still one stark contrast: Jerusalem deserved everything she received, but Jesus did not. He was one who knew no sin, but God made him to "be sin . . . so that in him we might become the righteousness of God" (2 Corinthians 5:21). From Jesus's judgment experience came salvation for God's sinful and miserable people.

So these words of sorrow in Lamentations 1 point the Christian believer to our Man of Sorrows. There we can find comfort for our sin and misery.

GOD'S COMFORT IN OUR SIN AND MISERY

Notice that the lament of chapter 1 ends in prayer. This is significant because it shows us what lament really is. Lament involves complaint, but it is not simply complaint. Lament is complaint directed toward God in prayer. Lament is saying, "Why, *oh Lord*? How long, *oh Lord*?" If all we do is complain when sorrow comes, then we're just complaining—but if we direct that complaint to God, then we are lamenting.

Lamentations 1 is depressing because of the refrain "there is none to comfort." Yet by the end of the chapter, the people have turned to God in a prayerful lament because he is the only one who can help. The prayer of lament in Lamentations 1 answers the question where do you go in your sin and misery when you've nowhere to go? You turn to God in prayer because only he is the one who can help.

More specifically, you turn to Jesus Christ, the great Comforter. For Jesus says,

> "Come to me, all who labor and are heavy laden, and I will give you rest. Take my yoke upon you, and learn from me, for I am gentle and lowly in heart, and you will find rest for your souls. For my yoke is easy, and my burden is light." (Matthew 11:28–30)

The reason Jesus can offer such rest for weary sinners like us is because the experience of Lady Zion finds its fulfillment in his person and work. Many of the experiences of the lonely woman city are seen in the lonely man Jesus Christ. The ghastly horror of war in Lamentations depicted in miniature the ghastly horror of hell Jesus experienced on the cross. But from his judgment experience came the salvation of God's people. This, then, is where we find comfort in our sin and misery, in the Man of Sorrows and our great Comforter, Jesus Christ.

DISCUSSION *10 MINUTES*

Lamentations 1 details Jerusalem's suffering in many ways: lonely and betrayed, restless and under distress, without a human comforter and before a silent God. Which of these resonate with your experience the most?

In Jerusalem's lament, she had no one to comfort her, but as the New Testament people of God, we do have a comforter in our misery over sin. How does knowing that Jesus has experienced suffering help you look to him for comfort?

Lesson

EXERCISE

LEARNING TO LAMENT, TURNING TO JESUS

20 MINUTES

In the beatitudes, Jesus says, "Blessed are those who mourn, for they shall be comforted" (Matthew 5:4). The book of Lamentations shows us how we have hope when we take our sin seriously enough to lament. We discover the comfort that God offers those who mourn.

PART 1: IDENTIFYING OUR ALTERNATIVES TO LAMENT. If we are honest, most of us don't usually lament our sin. Instead, we might respond to our sin and misery in many other ways.

The chart below describes alternatives to lamenting our sin.

- Check off the things that you do.
- Circle the one you'd say is your default pattern.
- Think about a recent time you engaged in one of these behaviors:
    - What were the circumstances?
    - Put it in your own words—what might you have said to yourself or somebody else?

Alternatives to Lament:	
We downplay or minimize our sin: *It's not that big a deal . . .*	We complain to others, whine, or gossip: *Can you believe how bad I have it? . . .*
We blame shift or make excuses for our sin: *It's not my fault . . .*	We get stuck and resign ourselves to ongoing sin: *Things are never going to change . . .*
We plan and strategize our own way to "solve it" out of self-reliance: *I can fix this by . . .*	We are paralyzed by overwhelming shame: *I am a terrible, unlovable person . . .*

PART 2: TURNING TO JESUS. Unlike Lady Jerusalem who had "none to comfort her," we live in light of Jesus—the one who stood in our place and went into exile for us on the cross. This gospel gives us freedom to be honest about our sin and to turn to Christ—our only source of comfort in our sin and misery.

Read through the following ways that the gospel changes how we respond to our sin and misery.

- Which do you most want to grow in?
- Where do you already see the gospel taking root in your life?
- Look up at least one of the Bible passages.

It's not that big a deal . . .	*Can you believe how bad I have it? . . .*
My sin is such a big deal that the Son of God had to die for it. Yet God's love for me is so great that he sent his Son to the cross. I have a daily need to repent and believe the gospel. Look up 1 John 1:5–9.	The fact that Lamentations is included in the Scriptures gives me permission, and even a model, for bringing my complaint directly to God (instead of just complaining). In prayer, I can be honest with my Father about my suffering and misery, even if I brought it upon myself. Since Jesus himself was a man acquainted with sorrows, I can find great comfort in him. Look up 1 Peter 5:7, 10.

It's not my fault . . . The gospel allows me to own up to my sin. I can readily admit my mistakes and failures because I have an unwavering righteousness before God. Instead of making excuses for myself, I can look to Jesus and receive his perfect record. Look up 2 Corinthians 5:19, 21.	*Things are never going to change . . .* God loves me too much to leave me in my sin. His zeal is to cleanse me, sanctify me, and present me without blemish or wrinkle to his Son, our great bridegroom. Also, God not only cares about me, but he cares too much about his Son—who died to pull me out of sin—to simply leave me stuck in my sin. Look at how Christ loves the church in Ephesians 5:25–27.
I can fix this by . . . As a child of God, I'm called out of self-reliance and into greater dependency on God for all my needs. In fact, the Spirit is at work to enable me to cry out, "Abba Father," and turn to him in prayer. My Father's ear is bent toward me, attentive to my needs and cries for help. Look at Jesus's call to abide in John 15:5. Look at Paul's encouragement to pray in Romans 8:12–15.	*I am a terrible, unlovable person . . .* Jesus took the things from my past and from myself that fill me with guilt and shame, and put them to death on the cross. He now draws me to himself—he is a shield about me, my glory, and the lifter of my head (Psalm 3:3). Look up Colossians 2:13–14.

When the group is ready, share some of your responses. How does applying the gospel change how you relate to God in light of your sin and misery?

WRAP-UP AND PRAYER *10 MINUTES*

In Lamentations chapter 1, God's silence suggests his absence. But as the New Testament people of God, we have received the Holy Spirit—so we are never forsaken. We can pray knowing that our Father's ear is bent toward us. In this time of prayer, you are invited to bring your complaints to God in lament. Ask the Holy Spirit to make real to you the comfort and presence of our Savior. And thank God for his gospel that delivers us out of sin and misery.

Lesson

3

STANDING WHERE THE FIRE HAS ALREADY BEEN

BIG IDEA

As followers of Jesus, our lament over the consequences of sin needs to include both repentance and trust in his merciful provision of rescue.

BIBLE CONVERSATION *20 MINUTES*

In Lamentations 2, the lament of God's people over the destruction of Jerusalem and the temple continues. Things are so bad that by verse 11, the prophet is no longer able to remain a detached commentator or observer—he himself begins to weep over what he sees. Verses 11–17 show the prophet's emotional response to the destruction of Jerusalem.

The prophet then encourages Lady Zion to keep weeping and to cry out to God (vv. 18–19). The chapter concludes with Lady Zion's lament (vv. 20–22). For the first time, she speaks and complains directly to God about what he has done to her.

Have someone read **Lamentations 2** aloud, or have a few readers take turns. Then discuss the questions below:

Lady Zion is experiencing God's just punishment of her sins. How does her punishment illustrate how truly horrific our sin is to God?

What is the prophet's emotional response to the destruction of Jerusalem?

In what ways is your emotional response toward suffering similar or different from the prophet's?

****

Now take turns reading the article aloud, switching readers with each paragraph. Then discuss the questions that follow.

Lesson

LIVING IN BETWEEN GOD'S PAST AND FUTURE DAYS OF JUDGMENT

5 MINUTES

These days, God's promised judgment of sin does not really evoke fear in the hearts of people. If they believe that he exists at all, they tend to think of him as a benevolent, old grandfather, who wishes no harm on anyone and who would alleviate all the suffering in the world if he could. What a different picture we have here in Lamentations 2!

In this chapter, God is portrayed as an angry, merciless God who comes to destroy his people, their city, and their temple because of their sin. He leaves them scattered and shattered, sitting in silence and sackcloth. God is the enemy-warrior, the temple-demolisher, and the city-destroyer.

As we encounter these words of lament, let's consider how we are to understand and apply Lamentations 2 as New Testament Christians. Let's focus on how the chapter begins and ends, with a reference to the day of God's anger.

REPENT NOW AND BE SPARED

In the Old Testament, there are several "judgment days," each of which previews the one final day of God's judgment in some way. These include the expulsion from Eden, the flood, the destruction of Sodom and Gomorrah, the Passover night in Egypt, the crossing of the Red Sea, the conquest of Canaan. Like the destruction of Jerusalem and the temple in Lamentations, all these serve as "judgment days" that foreshadow the final day of God's anger.

Our response to this coming day should be similar to that of the old men and young women in Zion—we should express repentance in light of it. They expressed repentance *after* the day, when it was too late; but it was the right response. We should express repentance *ahead* of the day, while it is not too late.

TRUST IN GOD'S SALVATION

In chapter 1, we saw how Jerusalem's sin and misery point ahead to Jesus. The same is true again in chapter 2, especially with respect to the temple and its destruction.

God's temple in Jerusalem symbolized God's presence with his people and typified Jesus—Immanuel, "God with us" (Matthew 1:23). Indeed, speaking of his own death, Jesus identified himself as the temple of God.[1] So we can see how the temple's destruction on the day of God's anger foreshadowed Jesus's experience of the day of God's anger.

Jesus's experience on the day he died recalls much of what we see in verses 1–10. On Calvary, Jesus was surrounded by the "dark cloud" of God's judgment (v. 1). His splendor was "cast down" (v. 1) from heaven to earth; in fact, even lower—it was cast down to Sheol. On the cross, God treated Jesus "without mercy" (v. 2) as he poured out his "fury like fire" upon him (v. 5). Jesus was, like the temple on Judah's judgment

1. John 2:19

day, "laid waste" (v. 6). Like the altar of sacrifice, he was "scorned" (v. 7), and like the sanctuary, he was "disowned" by God (v. 7).

Jesus was delivered into the hands of the enemy—the Jews, the Romans, Pilate and Herod—and yes, even into the hands of God. Indeed, God was determined to lay him to "ruin" (v. 8).[2] Like the walls of the city, Jesus "lamented" and "languished," as he hung on the cross (v. 8). In his darkest hour, he was given "no vision from the LORD" (v. 9), as he cried out, "My God, my God, why have you forsaken me?" (Matthew 27:46).

God's rejection of Jerusalem and her temple foreshadowed his rejection of Jesus—*the* Temple. Jerusalem's hell*ish* experience, in which they were brought down, down, down to the dust of the earth, was Jesus's *hell* experience, in which he was brought down, down, down to the abyss of Sheol.

For Jerusalem-Judah it was all deserved—not a bit of it unjust; but for Jesus it was all undeserved—not a bit of it just. And yet there was no actual injustice because Jesus willingly died as the innocent substitute for his guilty people:

> For our sake he made him to be sin who knew no sin, so that in him we might become the righteousness of God. (2 Corinthians 5:21)

And from that dark and damnable day came light and salvation. That day of darkness for Jesus has become our day of light; that day of God's judgment for Jesus has become our day of salvation. So we ought to put our trust in that past day of salvation as we wait for the future day of judgment.

---

2. See Acts 2:23.

If we do put our trust in Jesus, then that future day of God's judgment need not induce any terror or evoke any fear. Jesus has already anticipated it for us; he's already undergone it for us.

In 2009, the State of Victoria, in Australia, experienced the worst fires in the nation's history—173 people died in what is now known as the "Black Saturday bushfires." I remember watching the news and hearing the amazing testimony of a couple who escaped the fires. They literally had to flee their house with just a few belongings. They jumped in their car and headed down the road, only to find the fires coming at them from the side and behind and in front. Just as they thought there were going to be engulfed, the husband saw a piece of burnt ground off the side of the road. In complete desperation, he swerved on to it and sat there waiting for the fires to come. The ground was still so hot that the car tires blew as they waited. But the fires never touched them because they were parked where the fires had already been.

That is what the cross of Christ means to us. It is the place where the fire of God's future judgment has already been. And if our trust is in Christ and his death on the cross for us, we need not fear the future judgment.

DISCUSSION *10 MINUTES*

What does it mean to express repentance as we look ahead to the day of God's judgment? What might this look like in our lives?

Looking back at the past day of God's judgment, what strengthens your faith and helps you trust in Jesus's salvation?

Lesson

POUR OUT YOUR HEART

20 MINUTES

Just like Lady Jerusalem was encouraged to bring her lament to the Lord, we too are invited to "Cry out" and "Pour out your heart" to the Lord. A lament spoken to God is an exercise of faith. You tell about your suffering and misery, knowing that God listens and cares.

For this exercise, you will work on your own to compose a short, personal lament that you will pour out to God. Your lament might be about your sins or about the effects of sin you see causing misery around you. You can look at Psalm 32 as an example.

Follow the instructions below. When you finish, you won't be asked to share your lament with the group unless you want to, but you will have an opportunity to talk about the process of lamenting.

COMPOSE YOUR LAMENT. Write a few lines of personal lament. You might begin like the lament begins in verse 20, "Look, O LORD, and see," and then describe your experience or feelings. Also, like Lady Jerusalem brought her raw, unfiltered questions to the Lord, you might ask your difficult questions. Use the space below to write out your lament:

PRAY YOUR LAMENT. Now spend time with God in personal, silent prayer. Take the words you wrote and tell them to your Father, knowing that he hears and cares. Remember that Jesus has willingly stood as our substitute and taken God's judgment for our sin on himself. In Christ we can approach God's throne with confidence, even in our lament, knowing that our Father bends his ear toward us in love.

When the group is ready, discuss your time of lament. How did it feel to write and pray?

How might the practice of lament be good for you, either individually or as a group?

WRAP-UP AND PRAYER *10 MINUTES*

Finish with group prayer. You might include some laments from the exercise if any were shared with the group.

Lesson

4

A JOURNEY TOWARD HOPE

BIG IDEA

Those who suffer are called to place their hope in the Lord, for their suffering is temporary but his love for them is eternal—great is his faithfulness.

BIBLE CONVERSATION *20 MINUTES*

As Jerusalem's lament continues in Lamentations 3, the voice of the speaker changes. Chapters 1–2 are from the voice of Lady Zion. In chapter 3, the speaker identifies himself as "the man who has seen affliction," whom we'll also refer to as the prophet.

The afflicted man is one of the people living in Judah. In verses 1–18, he is speaking as a personified representative of the nation's suffering. His voice is their voice, and he represents them. However, the prophet is also distinct from the people. He teaches them how to endure suffering, instructing them in his role as prophet.

Similar to chapter 2, this chapter again opens with the Lord's relentless, violent attacks on "the man" (vv. 1–18).[1] What's interesting this

1. See also Lamentations 2:1–10.

time is that God is not named until verse 18; he is simply referred to as "he," which heightens the estrangement between God and this man. But in verse 18, the prophet does name God, and that is when things begin to change.

Have someone read **Lamentations 3:1–24** aloud, or have a few readers take turns. Then discuss the questions below:

In verses 1–6, God is portrayed as a harsh shepherd. Consider the imagery here—what is God like in this lament? How does that contrast with scriptural images of the Good Shepherd?

How does the lament change when the speaker names God in verse 18?

****

Now take turns reading the article aloud, switching readers with each paragraph. Then discuss the questions that follow.

Lesson

GREAT IS THY FAITHFULNESS

5 MINUTES

ALL HAIL THE POWER OF JESUS'S NAME

The afflicted man's journey from the darkness of despair to the light of hope in Lamentations 3 is of significance for every Christian. As sinful people living in a fallen world that is under the power of the devil, we may suffer for our own sin, like this representative Judahite man did; or we may suffer for some providential reason, like Job did. Or we may suffer for what others have done to us, like Joseph did. But whatever our experience of suffering, and whatever reason behind our suffering, we can identify with the experience of this man of affliction, at least to some extent.

Suffering of whatever kind—spiritual, physical, psychological, emotional—can leave our soul feeling embittered and bowed down. We can feel bereft of peace and happiness. Our strength and energy can wither inside us as prolonged suffering wears on our souls. And we can feel like the hope that God once blessed us with is now dead. When we suffer, we can feel like God has withdrawn from us, or we can be tempted to withdraw from him. God can feel distant and nameless.

But the way out of such despair is given to us in the last word of verse 18: When the man reaches his lowest point in the dark, he finally names God in the dark. In the darkness of his despair, he names Yahweh, his covenant Lord, the one who providentially brought him into the despair.

This is the turning point for the man in his lament. ***The way out of the darkness is to name God in the darkness.*** *Because when we're in the darkness and left with nothing, then we realize that God is the only one left to help us.* When we call upon God's name in the darkness of our despair, slowly the darkness begins to dissipate in the light of his presence.

When our daughter Leila died, we committed to singing these verses every night:

> The steadfast love of the LORD never ceases;
> his mercies never come to an end;
> they are new every morning;
> great is your faithfulness. (Lamentations 3:22–23)

There's something about naming God in the dark, recalling his character of love, mercy, and faithfulness that actually lifts you out of the darkness of despair and brings you into the light of hope.

God's steadfast love, his never-failing mercies, as well as his great faithfulness, form a trilogy of covenant terms connected to God's name.[2] This is what the man recalls: the essential goodness of God's character. Verse 23 provides a further qualification on God's mercies: They are new-morning mercies—a comforting, daily truth. The final line "great is your faithfulness" is the emphatic climax to the whole description of God's character. God's faithfulness is great because his love is steadfast, and his mercies are never ending.

---

2. See also Exodus 34:6–7.

When we name God, we call upon his character of steadfast love and never-ending mercies, and we are not consumed. When we name God, we are recalling and affirming his covenant faithfulness. All hail the power of Yahweh's name!

HOW SWEET THE NAME OF JESUS SOUNDS

As New Testament Christians, we call on God through the name of his Son, Jesus Christ. And chapter 3 provides a beautiful foreshadowing of Jesus through this "man of affliction." Though Jesus knew no sin, he experienced many of the things this man of affliction experienced in Lamentations 3.

As both a representative for the people and a prophet distinct from the people, Jesus saw affliction under the rod of God's wrath on the cross. He was driven and brought into the darkness of Gethsemane and Golgotha. God turned his hand against him by abandoning him to cruel men.

God made him dwell in darkness, like the dead of long ago, as he lay in death's dark shadow for three days. God walled him about so that there was no escape from his enemies. God shut out his cry of dereliction on the cross, providing him with no answer. God's arrows were fatal for him.

He became the object of scorn, a laughingstock and mocking song by all peoples, including his own. His soul was bereft of peace and he forgot happiness. His splendor and glory perished on the cross as he voluntarily gave up his life. He experienced affliction and homelessness throughout his life, all the way up to his death—the wormwood and the gall were his bitter food. His soul was bowed down within him.

And yet, in the darkness of despair on the hill of Golgotha, Jesus called to mind—consciously, deliberately, actively—the covenant faithfulness of God in the word of God. Each of Jesus's statements from the cross revealed that his mind was fixed on God. He learned through bitter experience that God was all he needed because God was all he had. He could say from the cross, verse 24, "The Lord is my portion, therefore I will hope in him."

And now, since Jesus has made the journey from the darkness of despair to the light of hope through faith in his Father, we can also make that same journey through faith in him during our times of suffering. When we call upon his name in the darkness, then the light will begin to appear. All hail the power of Jesus's name!

It's why his name becomes sweet to us as well. Knowing that he knows what it is to suffer, under the burden of sin, under the common curse for sin, the sound of Jesus's name becomes sweet in our suffering. We have a Savior who knows what it is to suffer and yet he hoped in God in the midst of his suffering. And united to that same Savior by faith, our hope in God can be rekindled.

DISCUSSION *10 MINUTES*

Describe a time you have named God in the darkness of suffering—what difference did recalling his character make? What difference could it make in your current suffering?

How does the name of Jesus become sweeter because he knows what it is to suffer?

NAMING GOD IN THE DARKNESS

20 MINUTES

The turning point in Lamentations 3 is when the afflicted man names God in the dark. When we name God in the darkness of our despair, we are calling on his covenant character: his steadfast love, his never-ending mercies, his great faithfulness. We are calling on him to act upon his character and bring us through the grief and the suffering so that we might experience his steadfast love.

As a way of "naming God in the dark," this exercise will walk you through doing these activities individually:

1. *Remember* your afflictions, your bitterness, what weighs heavy on your soul (vv. 19–20).
2. Intentionally and deliberately *call to mind* God's character (vv. 21–23).
3. *Write* a prayer, naming God in the darkness of your suffering.

Then your group will have an opportunity to talk about this experience of "naming God in the dark."

REMEMBER MY AFFLICTION! As we begin our exercise, it might be helpful for you to consider an area of suffering or grief you are experiencing. It can be large or small, acute or persistent. Write a brief description of it.

BUT THIS I CALL TO MIND. Read the verses below to "call to mind" God's covenant character, or feel free to look up others.

- **Exodus 34:6:** The Lord passed before him and proclaimed, "The Lord, the Lord, a God merciful and gracious, slow to anger, and abounding in steadfast love and faithfulness."
- **Psalm 36:5–7:** Your steadfast love, O Lord, extends to the heavens, your faithfulness to the clouds. Your righteousness is like the mountains of God; your judgments are like the great deep; man and beast you save, O Lord. How precious is your steadfast love, O God! The children of mankind take refuge in the shadow of your wings.
- **Micah 7:18–19:** Who is a God like you, pardoning iniquity and passing over transgression for the remnant of his inheritance? He does not retain his anger forever, because he delights in steadfast love. He will again have compassion on us; he will tread our iniquities under foot. You will cast all our sins into the depths of the sea.
- **1 John 4:9–10:** This is how God showed his love among us: He sent his one and only Son into the world that we might live

> through him. This is love: not that we loved God, but that he loved us and sent his Son as an atoning sacrifice for our sins. (NIV)

WRITE A PRAYER. In your prayer . . .

1. recall who God is, in particular his steadfast love, never-ending mercies, and great faithfulness.
2. ask him to act upon his character and bring you through grief or suffering.

You can jot notes or write out your prayer in the space provided.

When your group is ready, gather back together. Discuss your experience of naming God in the dark. How could this be helpful to you?

What challenges or barriers do you face in naming God in your despair?

WRAP-UP AND PRAYER *10 MINUTES*

Finish with group prayer. Remember God's steadfast love, never-ending mercies, and great faithfulness. Ask him to act according to his character in the areas of suffering you experience.

Lesson

5

THE CUP SHALL PASS

BIG IDEA

God's judgment was devastating, but it is complete. Christ drank the cup of God's wrath for us, and he offers us instead the cup of life and salvation.

BIBLE CONVERSATION *20 MINUTES*

In the lament of chapter 4, the content is quite dark and heavy—the horrors of war. The personification is stripped away—we no longer have the voice of Lady Zion or the afflicted man. Here the prophet begins to speak in a matter-of-fact fashion about the horrors Jerusalem-Judah experienced in the Babylonian siege and its eventual destruction. The bulk of the chapter focuses on the impact of God's judgment, the aftereffects of the destruction on the community and its leadership. But it ends with a ray of hope that the destruction is complete and the exile will soon be over.

Chapter 4 has a simple outline:

1. Bad news: God's judgment is devastating (vv. 1–20)
2. Good news: God's judgment is finished (vv. 21–22)

Have someone read **Lamentations 4:1–22** aloud, or have a few readers take turns. Then discuss the questions below:

What is your emotional response to reading about the devastating suffering Jerusalem endured? How has that changed (or not) over the four chapters of the study so far?

If you could ask God a question that arises for you from reading this passage, what would it be?

****

Now take turns reading the article aloud, switching readers with each paragraph. Then discuss the questions that follow.

Lesson

THE DEVASTATING EFFECTS OF GOD'S JUDGMENT

5 MINUTES

Hell is not really a subject that many people in our society take seriously anymore. We tend to ignore it or minimize it or joke about it. The Bible, however, speaks about hell in frank and candid terms.

This is seen most clearly in the teachings of Jesus. Jesus spoke about hell more than he did about heaven. And when he spoke about it, he didn't mince his words—he spoke candidly, directly. For Jesus, hell is real and a reality that we must all face up to. So, despite our society ignoring it, minimizing it, or joking about it, Jesus calls us to take hell seriously.

Now, if there's one thing that brings the topic of hell back on our radar, it's the event and experience of war. That's no less true when it comes to Lamentations 4—because we have here the terrible horrors of war. In Lamentations 4, the horrors of the aftermath of war point to the horrors of hell for condemned sinners.

BAD NEWS: GOD'S JUDGMENT IS DEVASTATING (VV. 1–20)

Lamentations 4 provides one of the most vivid shadows of hell in the Old Testament. And such, it also presents us with a truly hopeless situation: Judah is left "without hope and without God in the world" (Ephesians 2:12 NIV). And it's the same for us: As sinners living in God's world, before we were saved, we were under God's wrath; we were "without hope and without God in the world."

The terrifying descriptions of Judah's day of destruction are paralleled and heightened by Jesus in the New Testament. Jesus describes hell as a place of "outer darkness," where there is "weeping and gnashing of teeth" (Matthew 8:12). He describes hell as the place "where their worm does not die and the fire is not quenched" (Mark 9:48). In the parable of the rich man and Lazarus in hell, the picture is one of torment and thirst.[1]

Though the images are metaphorical—since darkness and fire cannot coexist, nor worms and fire—they are not fantastical. Rather, they serve as symbols of greater realities—too horrific fully to reveal this side of the final judgment. Together, the images convey hell to be a real place of eternal torment and pain.

All this makes us ask, If this is the fate of sinners headed for God's wrath, what is our hope? It's the question Jerusalem-Judah was asking themselves in their bleak situation under God's judgment. The closing verses provide the hope they needed to hear: God's judgment is finished.

1. Luke 16:19–31

GOOD NEWS: GOD'S JUDGMENT IS FINISHED (VV. 21–22)

The chapter ends with a final climactic reversal, but one which has a surprising twist: Justice will be executed on Judah's enemy, Edom. Edom was one of Judah's main enemy aggressors throughout her history[2] but especially so at her destruction by the hand of the Babylonians.[3]

The "cup" stands as a metaphor for the wrath of God. The imagery here is that of the cup being passed from one lady nation to another. The cup of judgment that Lady Edom had made Lady Zion drink will now be passed back to her to drink. Lady Zion can take heart that her punishment is complete—she has already drunk the bitter cup of God's wrath in the destruction of Jerusalem and the exile to Babylon. But the cup of God's wrath awaits Edom.

The word *accomplished* here is significant—it means "finished, done, completed, ended." The good news for Judah is that she has served her time in exile; she has completed her 70-year punishment, and God will soon bring her back to the promised land—he will keep her in exile no longer. In other words, Lamentations 4 ends with the good news that God's judgment is finished.

CHRIST DRANK THE CUP FOR US

All of this foreshadowed the payment Christ would make when he went into exile on the cross to release us from being under God's wrath and to change our destiny from that of hell to that of heaven. Lamentations 4 connects to Christ when we consider this image of drinking the cup of God's wrath. In Gethsemane, Jesus pleaded with

---

2. Numbers 20:18–21

3. See Psalms 83:1–8; 137:7–9; Ezekiel 25:12–14; 35:5–6; Amos 1:11–12; Obadiah 1:5–7, 10.

his Father to "let this cup pass from me" (Matthew 26:39). He was speaking of the cup of God's wrath for the sins of his people that would be poured out on him on the cross. Yet in submission to his Father's will, Jesus chose to drink that cup.

As he endured the wrath of God for three hours in the darkness, he drank the cup of God's wrath down to its last dregs. His cry, "It is finished!" was a fitting finale on that day of the Lord's anger.

However, this is not the only "cup" of God's wrath in the New Testament. The apostle John in Revelation indicates that there yet remains another cup of God's wrath to be drunk by the nations on the final day of the Lord.[4] That future cup of God's wrath is what awaits all those who refuse to follow Jesus and instead worship the beast (Satan) and his image. But for those who believe in Jesus, the good news is great news: The cup of God's wrath is empty—it is finished!

And now, for those whose faith is in Christ, the only cup that awaits us is the cup of the new wine of Christ's kingdom, which we will drink on the day of the marriage supper of the Lamb.[5] For those who have accepted the wedding invitation, this is more than a ray of hope. And in the meantime, when we celebrate the Lord's Supper, we drink from a cup that gives us a foretaste of the marriage supper of the Lamb.

DISCUSSION *10 MINUTES*

The idea of hell is something folks tend to ignore, minimize, or joke about. In what ways do you see this in the communities you are a part of?

How is the "good news" that Jesus has taken the cup for us even better in light of the "bad news" of God's judgment?

---

4. Revelation 14:9–10
5. Revelation 19:6–8

Lesson 5

EXERCISE

HOW THE CUP OF SALVATION CHANGES OUR LIVES

20 MINUTES

Jesus drank the cup of God's wrath on our behalf; we now drink the cup of his salvation. In this exercise, you will think through the difference it makes that Jesus took the cup of wrath for you on the cross and has given you the free gift of the cup of salvation.

Look up the Bible verses in the chart below. Then jot down your thoughts about what Jesus has done in drinking the cup of wrath for you so you can now drink the cup of salvation.

	The Cup of Wrath	The Cup of Salvation
My Relationship with God	Ephesians 2:1–3	Ephesians 2:4–6
My Relationship with Others	Ephesians 2:11–12	Ephesians 2:13–19
My Response to Suffering	Hosea 7:14	Philippians 4:12–13
My Final Destiny	Hebrews 9:26	1 John 3:2

WRAP-UP AND PRAYER *10 MINUTES*

As you pray together, include praise and thanks that Jesus willingly drank the cup of God's wrath on your behalf. God's judgment was devastating, but it is complete!

Lesson

6

COMFORT IN SUFFERING

BIG IDEA

To understand God's love for us as we suffer, we need to look to Jesus—the founder and perfecter of our faith.

BIBLE CONVERSATION *20 MINUTES*

Chapter 5 is comprised of one long prayer by the community—the prophet does not interrupt to comment. The community's prayer begins with three exhortations: remember, look, and see. The people and prophet had earlier asked God to remember, to look, to see their affliction,[1] but so far God had not acted. In a sense, by repeating the imperatives here, the prophet gathers all the exhortations given in the book so far and encapsulates in a nutshell what the people want the Lord to do. It is a plea for him to act in the light of what he sees.

Right down to the final verse, chapter 5 is dark and despairing. It begins with the word *disgrace* in verse 1 and then unpacks that disgrace for nearly the whole chapter. However, it does end with some hope. As with chapters 3 and 4, a glimmer of hope emerges by the end

1. "Remember" was used in 3:19; "Look" and "see" were used in 1:11; 2:20; 3:50.

as the Lord's sovereignty is reaffirmed (5:19, 21). If the Lord is the one who has brought the destruction, then he is the one who can bring the restoration. Chapter 5 may be summarized as follows: The disgrace of suffering for a remnant people after experiencing devastating loss would be unbearable were it not for the fact that Yahweh, the covenant God, is still on his throne.

The chapter breaks down into this rough outline:

Disgrace for suffering (vv. 1–18)
Faith in waiting (vv. 19–22)

Have someone read **Lamentations 5:1–22** aloud, or have a few readers take turns. Then discuss the questions below:

What losses stand out to you in this chapter? How have you experienced loss in suffering? What losses do you most dread/fear/worry about?

What do you think the people most want from God at this point? How is that similar or different from what you most want from God in your suffering?

****

Now take turns reading the article aloud, switching readers with each paragraph. Then discuss the questions that follow.

Lesson

ARTICLE

LIVING IN LIMBO

5 MINUTES

All suffering involves loss at some level. I'm sure each of us can think of ways we have suffered loss in our lives, either through our own sins and faults, or through the sins and faults of others, or simply by the mere fact of living in a fallen world, under the common curse of death, as it groans for the new creation. Whatever our life circumstances, whatever our suffering, we can identify at some level with this basic truth: All suffering involves loss.

LIVING WITH LOSS (VV. 1–18)

This was the reality that Jerusalem-Judah experienced after the destruction of their city, temple, and nation at the hand of the Babylonians—they suffered terrible loss that went on for years and years. Their litany of losses spans the disgrace of economic, social, and national loss. God's people had quite literally lost everything—except for him.

If the litany of losses underlines anything, it's this: Sin *always* has miserable consequences that go on for generations. That's what the descendants of Judah were dealing with here: Their fathers sinned and they had to suffer the consequences. And it's the same for us. As a result of our sin or the sin of others, including Adam, we suffer consequences. And those consequences involve loss.

LIVING IN LIMBO (V. 20)

"Why do you forget us forever, why do you forsake us for so many days?" (v. 20). These questions, the last in the book, concern the length of time that the Lord has seemingly forgotten and forsaken his people. The writer uses the word *forever*. It is a reminder that in suffering the present can feel like an eternity.

The reason for the complaint is tied to the good news announcement at the end of chapter 4, that Zion's punishment is complete. The remnant community, therefore, rightly asks, if this is true, why are they still languishing in Babylon? If God has promised the end of their exile, why are they still living with loss?

These questions capture the element of waiting in suffering. It involves waiting—waiting for God to restore what has been lost, or destroyed, or left unfinished. All suffering involves living in limbo.

LIVING BY FAITH (VV. 19–22)

"But you, O Lord, reign forever; your throne endures to all generations" (v. 19) is an emphatic statement of trust in God's sovereignty right at the end of the book. Here is the great comfort in the midst of suffering: God is on his throne. God is ruling. He has never stopped ruling, even in the midst of our suffering.

Just think about how unbearable the devastating loss we experience in our suffering would be were it not for the fact that our covenant God is still on his throne. And his throne is indestructible; it endures forever, from generation to generation.

This is faith in action in the midst of suffering—a faith that clings to the truth that God is sovereign, and sovereign forever, and therefore sovereign across our lifetime. And if he is sovereign across our lifetime, then he is able to save in our lifetime, which brings us to the second way faith is expressed in these final verses.

Precisely because God is the one who brought the destruction on his people, he is also the one who can bring restoration for his people. The appeal "Restore us" is made to the Lord even though he has (up to this point) utterly rejected them. In other words, the people ask God to restore them to himself—despite the fact that he has led them into exile, and they remain under his righteous, and rightful, judgment.

This is a prayer to God in faith: The people believe that God will not reject them forever, as the prophet has already indicated.[2] The book of Lamentations thus ends on a note of faith—fragile faith, yes, but still faith in stark contrast with the despair with which the book began. The glimmering light of God's sovereignty (v. 19) and his salvation (v. 21) have begun to dispel the darkness of Jerusalem-Judah's exile, even though the dark night of God's wrath is not yet completely over. For now, the people must walk—and pray—by faith, not by sight. All suffering involves living by faith.

LOOKING TO JESUS—THE PIONEER OF OUR FAITH

Judah's experience of suffering the ongoing consequences of sin is the same for every believer living today. As Christians, we live under the common curse of sin and in a world still groaning from the aftereffects of Adam's fall.[3]

We live with loss—loss of respect and reputation as a result of our sin, or loss of relatives, relationships, health, or wealth as a result of living in a fallen world under the curse of sin, while this world groans waiting for the new creation.

---

2. Lamentations 3:31
3. Romans 8:22

And while we suffer this loss, we also live in limbo, between the already and the not yet, between the curse of the old age and the blessing of the new age. The punishment for our sin is complete—finished by Jesus on the cross—but we still live with sin's miserable consequences while we wait for the new heavens and the new earth.

So we still suffer. And when we do, we can experience, like Judah, the silence of God. He does not always answer our prayers immediately or clearly, making the encouragement to "wait upon the Lord" or to "walk by faith" all the more complex.

However, as believers we do have someone to look to in such times, someone who himself had to wait upon the Lord and walk by faith under the most intense suffering—we have Jesus Christ, the man of faith. In his earthly ministry, Jesus lived between the tension of the already and the not yet. He lived under the common curse of the old age as he sought to inaugurate, through his life, death, resurrection, and ascension, the blessing of the new age. He also knew what it was to live by faith under the peculiar curse of God for the sins of his people. In his life, he knew what it was to suffer loss while living in limbo.

On the cross, in those three hours of darkness, Jesus experienced the silence and abandonment of God, seen most clearly in his heart-wrenching question: "My God, my God, why have you forsaken me?" (Matthew 27:46, quoting Psalm 22:1). Quoted in isolation, Jesus's words may (mis)convey doubt or unbelief. But read in the context of Psalm 22, and in the context of Jesus's other statements from the cross, they convey faith grappling with the mystery of suffering.

Yes, Jesus felt abandoned by God for a time, but he also knew how Psalm 22 ended. He knew that God would not despise or abhor the affliction of the afflicted; that he would not hide his face from him forever but would hear him when he cried to him.[4] On the cross, Jesus

4. Psalm 22:24

did not waiver in his faith in God. Rather, he knew that God would not cast off forever. He knew that although God had caused grief for a time, he would show compassion again.[5] By faith, Jesus waited for the salvation of his God, knowing that it was good for a man to bear in his youth the yoke of punishment for sin.[6]

In short, Jesus knew what it was to suffer loss while living in limbo. He knew what it was to walk by faith between the already and the not yet throughout his life, and especially on the cross and in the "dead time" of the Sabbath day.

This is why the writer of Hebrews encourages us in times of trial and suffering to look to Jesus, "the founder and perfecter of our faith, who for the joy that was set before him endured the cross, despising the shame, and is seated at the right hand of the throne of God" (12:2). We are to look to Jesus in our time of suffering as the perfecter of faith because in his time of suffering he was the pioneer of faith—the man of faith par excellence.

DISCUSSION *10 MINUTES*

A common question to arise in suffering goes like this: "If God is both all-good and all-powerful, how could he have let this bad thing happen?" In light of what we've seen of God's sovereignty in Lamentations, how would you encourage a suffering friend who was asking that question?

What do you find most compelling about how Christ lifts the burden of sin and sorrow?

5. Lamentations 3:32
6. Lamentations 3:26–27

Lesson

EXERCISE

LOOKING TO JESUS IN OUR TIME OF SUFFERING

20 MINUTES

In Lamentations 5 we see the community of faith grappling with the mystery of suffering. And as Jesus hung on the cross and cried out, "My God, my God, why have you forsaken me?" (Matthew 27:46, quoting Psalm 22:1), we again see a picture of faith grappling with the mystery of suffering.

In this exercise, we are going to use Psalm 22 as a template for looking to Jesus in faith, as we ourselves grapple with the mystery of suffering. This exercise is designed to give form and expression to the messy reality of our experience of suffering.

Read Psalm 22:1–5, and then verse 19 (feel free to skim the rest as time allows).

- Notice the cries and questions of verses 1–2. The psalmist brings his experience of loss and limbo to the Lord.
- Then notice the "Yet" that begins verse 3, and the reflection of God's sovereignty. He is holy and seated on the throne.

- Finally, notice the cry for help in verse 19: "But you, O LORD, do not be far off! O you my help, come quickly to my aid!"

You are going to work through the questions on your own. Then your group will regather to discuss them.

BRINGING OUR EXPERIENCE OF LOSS AND LIMBO TO THE LORD (Psalm 22:1–2). Begin by considering some experience in which you are living in loss or limbo. For example, think of an area of unanswered prayer, a way in which you feel distant from the Lord, or an ongoing struggle where you "find no rest" (v. 2).

Jot down a brief description:

Now consider how you naturally respond to loss or limbo. Some common responses are fear, anger, depression, or escapism. What is your go-to or typical response to living in loss or limbo?

Write out a short description of how you typically think, feel, or act.

YET . . . : THE PRAYER OF FAITH (Psalm 22:3–5). Take time to remember what is true about God. Consider the one whose "throne endures to all generations" (Lamentations 5:19), and cling to the truth that God is sovereign across your lifetime.

- Look up at least one of these passages:
    - Psalm 22:3–5
    - Lamentations 5:19–22
    - Lamentations 3:22–24
- In your own words, write out a prayer or declaration of faith to God, focusing on what is always true about him.

"O YOU MY HELP, COME QUICKLY TO MY AID!" (Psalm 22:19). Take time to consider how Jesus has gone before you in his sufferings and can help you in your suffering. What would it look like for you to turn from your natural response to loss and limbo, and turn toward Jesus? How do you need the pioneer and perfecter of your faith to help you, to come to your aid? (Psalm 22:19). Remember, our goal is not to "do suffering better" on our own strength, but to know Christ in our suffering.

Finally, write out a prayer, asking the Holy Spirit to help you know Jesus in your suffering.

When the group is ready, talk about what truths about God you want to cling to as you endure life's suffering. How has this study as a whole helped you to know Christ in his suffering and to turn to him in your own?

WRAP-UP AND PRAYER *10 MINUTES*

As you pray together, include praise for the things that are eternally true of God and for the ways Jesus is the pioneer and perfecter of our faith. Pray for the ongoing work of the Spirit to help us look to Jesus and grow in faith, especially in times of suffering.

LEADER'S NOTES

LESSON 1: WHY LAMENTATIONS?

Lamentations is not a book of systematic theology. But it may be helpful to articulate a few theological points as a guide as you read the book. The leader's notes for this lesson are longer than those for the other lessons because they provide a theological overview of the entire book of Lamentations; feel free to refer back to this section in future lessons.

Sin Is Serious

It is hard to miss as you read through this book that God takes sin seriously. Verse after verse and chapter after chapter reveals that God brings his judgment on his people because of their sin.

Suffering Is a Consequence of Sin

Not only does the prophet define sin and then state the seriousness of sin, but he paints in vivid terms the suffering that results from sin. The city, temple, and people are in devastation and desolation as a result of their breach of covenant.

Providence of God

Despite Jerusalem-Judah's suffering resulting from their own fault, the writer of Lamentations makes it clear that none of what Judah has experienced has occurred outside God's providence (God's control of all things) or purpose. Yes, he uses secondary agencies, like the foreign nations, but ultimately Jerusalem-Judah's misery has come about by divine providence. As we will see in chapters 1 and 2, God is most active in Judah's destruction. However, this does not render him unjust . . . .

Justice of God

While Lamentations pinpoints the ultimate cause of Judah's afflictions on God himself, the book does not even hint that God is somehow unjust or unrighteous in his providential dealings with the nation. God is just—Judah has only received what they deserved.

In this regard, there is no theological conundrum in Lamentations, as there is in the book of Job. There is no mystery to Judah's suffering. There is a simple cause-and-effect relation: Judah sinned, therefore Judah suffered. And in all this, God was just. The prophet acknowledges as much in 1:18: "The LORD is in the right, for I have rebelled against his word."

Faithfulness of God

Lamentations 1 and 2 provide no real comfort or hope for the people. The prophet accepts and acknowledges the justice of God's punishment on Jerusalem-Judah for her sins. This continues into chapter 3 through the lone voice of the afflicted man, the prophet himself.

Comfort and hope in suffering is found in the God who is sovereign over suffering. He is no vindictive tyrant, but the God whose love is steadfast and whose mercies are new every morning—great is his faithfulness (3:22). God is faithful to his character and to his covenant, and that is what provides the prophet with hope in a seemingly hopeless situation.

Comfort in Suffering

Acknowledging the providence of God in suffering is foundational to finding the necessary comfort to endure the suffering. Even though God's providential dealings with his people can be sore and severe at times, hope and comfort lie in the God of such providence. If God is the one who has brought the pain, then he is the one who can bring the relief. This is why throughout the book, even in the midst of his suffering, the prophet turns to God for help. In Lamentations, the people and the prophet are brought to an end of themselves so that they might find their comfort in God alone.

Prayers of Lament

Since God alone is the one who is able to deliver Jerusalem-Judah, it is to him that the people should pray. Lamentations teaches us what such prayer looks like in the face of sin and judgment—it is an honest wrestling with God in the midst of justified suffering for one's sin.

LESSON 2: WHO WILL SAVE US FROM JUDGMENT?

Some of the depictions of suffering in Lamentations are graphic. Such passages require you to "handle with care." Enter it prayerfully, and be attentive to the Holy Spirit as you listen to people discuss what they read. But know too that the Spirit may use passages like these to do a surprisingly helpful work in the hearts of his people.

If people in your group share things that are raw and personal, don't feel the need to correct them or sanitize what they share. Don't try to fix a complex and painful life experience; it's okay to leave things a little messy and unresolved. Your goal is not to make everything "okay"—it's to learn to lament, to bring your prayer to Jesus.

Poetic Form: One of the main poetic features of Lamentations is its acrostic structure. Each stanza begins with the next letter of the Hebrew alphabet. The book is comprised of five acrostic poems: Chapters 1–4 form four distinct acrostic poems, composed according to the twenty-two letters of the Hebrew alphabet. Chapter 5 forms a quasi-acrostic poem (it contains twenty-two verses but does not follow the order of the Hebrew alphabet).

Why use the acrostic form? What does an acrostic poem achieve? Well, if you think about it, it helps memorization by providing a logical order. It also provides aesthetic beauty. Most significantly, it provides completeness of thought on a particular subject. In other words, acrostic poems provide a comprehensive overview of an experience or a subject by covering it from A–Z and everything in between. In the case of Lamentations, the prophet aims to provide a comprehensive theology of suffering—an A–Z if you like—of what it means to suffer for one's sin under divine providence.

LESSON 3: STANDING WHERE THE FIRE HAS ALREADY BEEN

Chapter 2 is bookended by references to the day of Lord's anger (vv. 1 and 22). In between those references, especially in the first half of the chapter, we have the relentless actions of God, the angry, merciless warrior, wreaking destruction on his people and their city and their temple. As you read, notice how active God is in verses 1–8.

The prophet weeps like Lady Zion in chapter 1, but he has an even more violent reaction, vomiting his bile out on to the ground at the sight of infants and babies dying in the streets and on their mother's bosoms (2:11–12). Who can't be moved by such a description, seeing children suffer? This is the most moving and poignant aspect of any war, isn't it? The prophet's emotional response is understandable. And in his response, we begin to see that he is presented to us as a sympathetic prophet who feels the pain of his people and who wants to do something about it. But for now, there seems to be nothing he can do about it. Like those of us who don't know what to say when someone we care about is suffering, he asks, "What can I say . . . that I may comfort you?" (v. 13).

LESSON 4: A JOURNEY TOWARD HOPE

Poetic Form: The book of Lamentations is made up of five poems, and in this lesson we come to the third poem in chapter 3. The chapter may look longer than chapters 1–2, but actually it's the same length with versification that is different. The poem follows the acrostic pattern seen so far, only this time there is an added concentration of the acrostic: Each letter of the Hebrew alphabet is repeated at the beginning of three consecutive verses before the next letter begins the next three verses. So the acrostic is more concentrated in chapter 3.

In 3:1–17, a litany of statements concerning God's active involvement in the prophet's misery pour out like a cascading waterfall, one after the other, to the point where he concludes in verse 18: "My endurance has perished; so has my hope from the LORD." The situation has brought them to an end of themselves. And yet, ironically, in that moment of hopelessness, the prophet calls out to the one who has made him feel hopeless—he calls out to God himself: "Remember my affliction and my wanderings, the wormwood and the gall!" (v. 19). Why turn to the one who has brought him into his debilitating situation? Why hope in the one who has made him feel hopeless? The prophet's answer is clear: because God is faithful (v. 22).

Additional Verses for Exercise 4—Naming God in the Dark

- **Psalm 30:5:** For his anger is but for a moment, and his favor is for a lifetime. Weeping may tarry for the night, but joy comes with the morning.
- **Psalm 73:26:** My flesh and my heart may fail, but God is the strength of my heart and my portion forever.
- **Psalm 78:38:** Yet he, being compassionate, atoned for their iniquity and did not destroy them; he restrained his anger often and did not stir up all his wrath.

- **Isaiah 33:2:** O Lord, be gracious to us; we wait for you. Be our arm every morning, our salvation in the time of trouble.
- **Hebrews 10:23:** Let us hold fast the confession of our hope without wavering, for he who promised is faithful.

LESSON 5: THE CUP SHALL PASS

Edom is chosen here in 4:2–22 presumably because it represents the epitome of betrayal that Judah had experienced. Of all the nations that Judah looked to in vain for help to save them (v. 17), Edom represented their best hope, given their fraternal relation to Judah (Genesis 36). Edom comes from Esau and Judah from Jacob, and we remember that Esau and Jacob were twins. So the two nations were, in effect, "twins." Yet Esau-Edom did violence against his brother Jacob-Judah, betraying them into the hands of the Babylonians (Obadiah 10).

LESSON 6: COMFORT IN SUFFERING

The Bible teaches a number of truths that often appear to be in tension with one another—at least to our limited human understanding. For example, if God is sovereign and plans all things, are human beings still responsible for their actions? Or, in this case, if God is sovereign and good, why does he let bad things happen? In such theological dilemmas, we must let God's Word be our guide and submit to it, even when we don't quite understand it or an experience of suffering makes it confusing. Also, we should not let the difficult and confusing things in life keep us from believing the clear and simple things in God's Word. With respect to suffering, the Bible is clear: God is sovereign and all-powerful and plans everything that comes into our lives (Psalm 115:3)—yes, even the difficult things and tragedies. But the Bible is equally clear that God is loving, good, and kind in all his ways (Psalm 145:17)—so much so that whatever suffering he may bring into our lives, we can be sure that he has many good purposes for it, chiefly to conform us to the image of his Son (Romans 8:28–29). More broadly, just the fact that we live in a fallen world means that in God's providence we are susceptible to experiencing the fallout of Adam's sin. But as Christians we have the hope that one day, when Jesus returns, God is going to wipe away every tear, and death and suffering will be no more (Revelation 21:1–4).

Poetic Form: Chapter 5 doesn't follow the acrostic format as the other chapters do. It has the same number of verses as there are letters in the Hebrew alphabet, but the verses don't follow the Hebrew alphabet like the other chapters. The prophet deliberately breaks up the acrostic form to emphasize some of the atrocities that the people of Judah experienced. It's also the shortest chapter of the book. In this way, it creates an imbalance to the book as it sort of peters out at the end.

Now what do these observations communicate? Well, the length and structure of chapter 5 reveals that suffering does not always end in a neat and tidy way. You can't tie up suffering in a nice, perfect bow. Suffering is messy, and the messiness of the last poem as it deviates from the ordered acrostic pattern conveys this messiness. It also conveys that suffering is exhausting and can leave you unable to complete things as you wished.